HIDDEN
CREDIT REPAIR
SECRETS

7 Steps to Disputing a Debt and Winning

FRANCES B. WILLIAMS

Although the author and publisher have made every effort to ensure that the information in this book was correct at press time, the author and publisher do not assume and hereby disclaim any liability to any party for any loss, damage, or disruption caused by errors or omissions, whether such errors or omissions result from negligence, accident, or any other reason.

This book is designed to provide accurate and authoritative information about personal finance. Neither the author nor the publisher is engaged in the rendering of legal or accounting by publishing this book. If any such assistance is required, the services of a qualified professional should be sought. The author nor the publisher will not be held for any liability, loss, or risk incurred because of the use and applications of any of the information contained in this book.

While the author has made every effort to provide telephone number and internet addresses at the time of publication, neither the publisher nor the author assumes any responsibility for errors or for changes that occur after publication.

P.O. Box 440061 Houston, Texas 77244 1-855-855-6157
Ordering Information:
Quantity sales. Special discounts are available on bulk purchases by corporations, associations, and others. For details, contact the publisher at the address and phone number above.
Printed in the United States of America. ISBN 978-1545483817
Visit us on the web www.123creditconsultants.com

If you do not see any results from your disputing efforts or if you have questions that have not covered in this book, you need to seek professional credit restoration assistance from 123 Credit Resolution Consultants.

To my sweet grand nanny thank you for giving me my start. To my "little" brothers, Unk, Ma, and social media family thank you for all your support.

Contents

Introduction

"If you want to live a life you've never lived, you will have to do something that you've never done before. You can't expect different results from the same old habits."

- FRANCES B.

While I was on a date at a popular Mexican restaurant, I stood up to go grab a handful of napkins. As I am walking across the room, I glanced out of the window and saw my car being loaded onto the back of a tow truck. My heart felt like it was about to thump out of my chest because I realized that my car was being repossessed. My college textbooks, my backpack, my work badge, and other personal belongings were hauled away along with my car. I must say that day was one the most embarrassing days of my life.

For an entire year, my commute back and forth to work was a nightmare. After experiencing an embarrassing car repossession and losing my belongings, I soon realized that I no longer had dependable transportation to work. Since I no longer had a car, I had to rely on public transportation which added an extra four hours to my journey.

Each day, I walked two miles to the train and then rode two buses to work. After my work shift ended, I walked to the bus stop, sat and waited twenty minutes for the bus to arrive. I rode the bus from my job to the transfer station where I board a second bus to take me to downtown Houston. Once I arrived at downtown Houston, I waited ten minutes on the train to arrive and take me towards my condo. After riding the train towards my condo, I walked two miles to my house. For an entire year, regardless of the weather conditions, I traveled back and forth to work using public transportation in the rain, hail, sleet, and snow.

On top of adding four hours to my commute, I had to cope with two things: arriving to work late or arriving to work drenched from head to toe. Public transportation in Houston is not always 100 percent reliable which sometimes caused me to clock in at work late or not at all. Everyday cars drove by hitting potholes filled with water, splashing water all over me forcing me to arrive at work with wet clothes on. I must be honest and say that the struggle was real.

After being carless for an entire year, I managed to save up enough money for a down payment towards a new car. I did not have enough money saved to purchase a car in full, so I traveled to a local dealership to finance it. At that time, I did not understand credit reports, credit scores, etc. but I assumed that I would not have any issues financing a vehicle since I had a deposit. Even though I had $2,500 to use as a deposit towards a new car, I was given the disappointing news that they could not find a bank that would finance a car for me. The finance manager explained to me that my credit score was too low and I must improve my credit to qualify for a car loan.

So that day I began my credit journey. I decided that I was not going to pay anyone to repair my credit, so I decided to do my own research. I read articles online and watched videos on YouTube to figure out what I could do to boost my credit score.

With the money that I saved up, I decided to pay off collection accounts on my credit report. Like most people, I thought that after I paid the collection agencies, the negative accounts will be deleted from my credit report. So, I began to do just that; I called several collection companies and paid the balance in full. Then I contacted the hospital and asked for the phone number to their collection agency. I spoke to every creditor and collection agency on my credit and paid the balance in full. It really felt great to know that I was making steps towards improving my credit.

I really thought I was doing a great job repairing my credit until I checked my credit scores. To my surprise, my credit score decreased forty-something points. I was completely devastated, but I did not give up hope. I went back online to study different online articles and purchased a few books about repairing credit. I read through each book, compared the information, and highlighted everything. I followed the books' instructions step by step.

After two months of disputing and paying off collection accounts, I pulled up my credit scores again. I was heartbroken. My credit scores decreased from the five hundreds to the low four hundreds. My heart sunk into my stomach. It was at that very moment; I realized that I really did not understand the process as well as I thought. I felt hopeless! I made a lot of costly errors, wasted thousands of dollars, and successfully decreased my credit score.

Over the past few years, I spent countless hours, months, years, and thousands of dollars to learn about credit. I spent most of my studies not only learning about credit but understanding the topics that surround credit. I quickly learned that repairing credit is no easy tasks.

If you want to be efficient at restoring your credit, you must understand the reason why people have bad credit. From my experience, bad credit is caused by two things: insolvency issues and the lack of credit education. In short, many people are not financially prepared for the unexpected especially if the circumstances are out of their control.

Like many people in America, I did not have wealthy parents and grew up in a single parent household. I was not educated about the importance of credit in middle school, high school, or college. To make matters worse, my immediate family had bad credit as well.

Credit is a taboo topic that society has coupled in with other taboo topics such as disabilities, mental illness, sexism, racism, religion, and politics. My purpose of this book is to encourage people to make smart financial decisions, understand the importance of credit, and make the topic of credit conversational and less taboo. This book will create an opportunity you to have access to accurate information that can be used to understand credit better, teach your children about credit, and help end the never-ending cycle of bad credit in our communities.

Before I start revealing my hidden credit repair secrets, I would like to help you start your journey with a new perspective. I know how difficult it is to go through your credit journey. To be honest, many people do not want to evaluate their credit report and credit scores because it is disheartening. I understand that reviewing your credit report is like giving yourself a constant reminder about a dark time that you experienced in your past.

Many people suffer from horrible credit scores because he or she encountered difficulties in their life that were outside of their control. I want to remind you that we are all human beings. We are not perfect, and we all go through things in life that are unexpected. Losing a loved one, getting divorced, becoming ill, and being fired from your job is a part of this roller-coaster journey many refer to as life. I encourage you to tackle your credit situation with confidence. Now it is time for you to begin your own credit journey. Grab a pen, paper, and a highlighter and turn to page one to begin your credit journey. I look forward to hearing your success stories.

Credit Basics: Credit Scores, Report, and Bureaus

Credit Basic Introduction

There are many misinterpretations and myths about credit. The most common myth that people believe is that their credit reportsautomatically report information that is up to date and accurate which is false. The credit bureaus do not review your credit report line by line to make sure the information on your credit report is correct. The credit bureau's primary goal is to gather data and information about you (the consumer) and sell the information to those who request it (lenders, employers, etc.).

To give you a better understanding of how credit reporting works we will compare your credit profile to your fingerprints. Although others may have a similar fingerprint pattern, no one will ever have the exact same fingerprint pattern like yours. The same example holds true about your credit report. Even though a friend or relative may have similar accounts on their credit report, their credit scores will not be the same exact number as yours. Therefore, the solutions that you use to repair and rebuild your credit report may not work for someone else.

Utilize the information and tools in this book to aid you in creating your own dispute strategy to R.R.R., Review, Repair, and Re-build, your credit profile.

In the upcoming chapters, I am going to abolish many myths about credit by educating you about the foundation of credit, how credit can be useful, and how to use credit to move your life in a new direction.

If you have been a victim of an identity thief, filed bankruptcy, or faced foreclosure, you can restore your credit profile and have second chance at good credit.

One of the major keys to having excellent credit and financial freedom is education. Once you understand how credit works, you will be able to identify what prevented you from having excellent credit previously and avoid having poor credit in the future.

Studying and repairing your credit is not an overnight process. Many people enrolled in our credit repair program enrolls for an average of 6-9 months and typically see changes within 30-45 days. If you follow the information in this book, you will see changes as well.

Credit Scores

A credit score is a number generated by a mathematical formula that is meant to predict creditworthiness. Credit scores range from 300-850. The higher your score is, the more likely you are to get a loan. The lower your score is, the less likely you are to get a loan. If you have a low credit score and you do get approved for credit, then your interest rate will be much higher than someone who had a better credit score and borrowed money. Therefore, having a high credit score can save you thousands of dollars over the life of your mortgage, auto loan, or credit card.

Credit Bureau History

A credit bureau is a company that houses your information and sales it to those who request it. Each credit bureau provides information such as your personal information, account details, payment history, and accounts on a comprehensive statement referred to as your credit report. Even if the information on your credit report is inaccurate, the credit bureaus sell your information to creditors, employers, and lenders.

Lenders must become a paying member of the credit bureau to get a record of how you paid or is paying your creditors. Most of the information on your credit report is from creditors that you had or have opened an account with or provided information to when you applied for credit.

Many people believe that the credit bureaus are the ones who turn them down for credit when in all actuality it is the members (aka lenders) who turn you down for credit. The credit bureaus report information that is provided to them.

Another popular myth about the credit bureau is that the credit bureaus are the ones who removes information from your credit reports but this is not true.

The credit bureaus are not authorized to remove information from your credit report unless the collection agency or creditor contacts the bureaus to have the information remove or if the information on your report violations your consumer rights.

The credit bureaus cannot remove any information from your credit report unless they have permission from the collection agency or creditor. So, if you send a dispute to the credit bureau(s) regarding a collection account on your credit report, the credit bureaus are going to contact the collection agency to verify the information. If the collection agency does not respond to the dispute, then the collection account is removed from your credit report. If the collection agency replies and says the information is correct then the information will remain on your credit report. So, in sum, the credit bureaus act on behalf of the creditor or collection agency not on behalf of the consumer.

The credit bureaus can remove an account from your credit report if it violates your consumer rights. Congress has many laws they have passed to protect consumers in regards to their finances and credit. One of the most popular laws that relates to your credit, is the Fair Credit Reporting Act.

The Fair Credit Reporting act states that all the information on your credit report must be up to date, accurate, and verifiable information. So, if you send a dispute to credit bureaus to dispute a collection account, the credit bureaus will contact the collection agency to verify the information. If the collection agency does not respond to the credit bureau's dispute request for additional information, then the account has to be removed from your credit report. The reason the account has to be removed is because the information is unverifiable.

The dispute process can be a lengthy process since the credit bureaus have thirty days to respond to each dispute request and an additional fifteen days to send their dispute response in the mail to you. To save time when repairing your own credit, I highly recommend subscribing to a paid credit monitoring service so you can get an electronic alert and updated credit report versus waiting an additional fifteen days for the response to come to you via mail.

Yes, there are a lot of free websites where you can get updates regarding your credit most of them do not give you access to all of your credit reports just one or two credit bureaus. You need an updated credit report and scores from all three of the major three credit bureaus in order to have successful results from your credit repair efforts.

Most services can range anywhere between twenty to fifty dollars per month depending on which company you choose to subscribe too. Most of the companies all have similar features so there is no need to pay more than twenty dollars per month to access this information.

If you would like to save money and get a copy of your credit reports and credit scores from all three bureaus, I have a free credit score hack for you. Simply go online, open your web browser, and type in www.123creditconsultants.com/fcrnow in the search bar. From there you can gain access to my free credit report hack where you can get all three of your credit reports and scores for just one dollar. Simply follow the instructions to ensure you get a refund of your one dollar after you access and print your credit reports and scores.

If you visit the website address, I provided above, you will also have access to my most highly recommended credit monitoring service that I use to monitor my own credit. For less than twenty dollars per month, you will gain access to all three of your credit reports, your credit scores, identity thief protection, and more.

Credit Bureau's History

Before the credit bureaus existed, merchants and businesses would lend money to people who may need it only if they knew the person personally and if they had a good history with paying back other merchants. As you can imagine, many people were not able to borrow money if they were new to a town, had no history with local merchants, or if the merchant just did not know them.

A new solution to this problem was founded by local merchants who created an extensive list of people who borrowed money and did not pay them back. When requested, local merchants would share their list of high-risk people with other merchants.

As the population of the United States grew so did the demand for this valuable information. When the information was requested, merchants would send their report through automobile and/or train across America. As the popularity of this new system grew, more information was added to the reports which made the report became very problematic to update.

The solution to this problem created the birth of what we refer to now as the credit bureaus: Equifax, Experian, and Transunion. The credit bureaus, often referred to as the big three, was founded in the late 1800s.

Equifax was formally known as "Retail Credit Company." Retail credit company grew quickly, established offices across America, and shared information with anyone who requested it. The company used to collect information about every aspect of consumers life such as marriage troubles, jobs, school history, and political activities.

In 1970, the Fair Credit Reporting Act was passed that limited the amount of information that is shared and to whom it can share with. Up until the Fair Credit Reporting Act was passed, information was being stored in unethical ways and shared with anyone who requested it. The Fair Credit Reporting Act was passed to regulate and protect consumer's personal information and credit history.

Since Retail Credit Company's reputation was already at stake for sharing such personal information, they re-branded and changed their name to Equifax.

After their rebranding, Equifax stored information electronically and limited the amount of information that they collected and shared about consumers.

Transunion was founded in 1968 by Union Tank Car. Union Tank Car was a railroad company that acquired their parent company Transunion. Transunion created the Credit Bureau of Cook County manual that maintained over three million files in 400 file cabinets.

Transunion uses an electronic method to store and share consumer data and has over 250 offices across twenty additional countries.

Experian was the last of the big three companies to be found. Experian was founded in England in 1980s under the name CCN systems. Experian did not offer its services to the United States until 1996 when they purchased a company called TRW Information Systems. Experian is now in more than 30 countries and has offices across the world.

3 Major Credit Bureau's Contact Details

Equifax Information Services LLC

P.O. Box 740256 Atlanta, GA 30374
Telephone: 1-866-349-5191Online: www.equifax.com

TransUnion LLC Consumer Disclosure Center

Address: P.O. Box 2000,Chester, PA 19022
Telephone: 1-800-916-8800 Online: www.transunion.com

Experian National Consumer Assistance Center

Address: P.O. Box 2002,Allen, TX 75013
Telephone: 1-888-397-3742Online: www.experian.com

E-Oscar

efore we discuss disputing items on your credit report, we need to discuss the credit bureau's disputing process. The credit bureaus use a system called E-Oscar.

E-Oscar is a system the credit bureaus use to investigate credit disputes. The E-Oscar system also known as (the Online Solution forComplete and Accurate Reporting) began in 1993 and is owned by Experian, Equifax, Transunion, and Innovis. The E-Oscar system allows the credit reporting agencies to respond to consumer credit disputes automatically.

The system changes your consumer dispute to a two or three-digit code, and that code is used to explain your reason for the dispute. According to Leonard A. Bennett of Consumer Litigation Associates,the popularly used codes are:

- Not his/hers 30.5%
- Dispute present/previous accounts status/history 21.2%
- Disputes amount 8.8%
- Account closed by consumer 7.0%

Once a code is assigned to consumer's disputes, a two or three digit code is sent to the original creditor to verify. Then the lender just responds to the system as accurate or inaccurate, and the dispute response updates on the credit report.

Types of Credit

There are four different types of credit: secured credit, unsecured credit, installment credit, and non-installment credit.

Secured credit is a type of credit that is "secured" by collateral such as your car, your home, or your money. An example of secured credit would include but is not limited to a home loan, auto loan, pay day loan, or car title loan.

Unsecured credit is a type of credit that you can gain access too without any collateral. So, the lender or creditor will give youcredit solely based on your credit scores and income. An example of unsecured credit would include but is not limited to, an unsecured credit card, debt consolidation loan, or personal loan.

Installment credit is the type of credit and can be secured or unsecured loan. An installment loan monthly payment are typically the same amount of equal payments paid over a particular period of time such as auto loan, furniture loan, student loan, or personal loan.

Non-installment credit is similar to a postpaid account which is an account you pay for after service has been rendered. If you have a non-installment loan or account, you will typically receive a letter in your mailbox that says, "full payment due upon receipt." An example of a non-installment credit loan would be a furniture loan that offers no interest paid if the loan is paid in full within the first ninety days.

Although this section of the book is to educate you about the basics of credit, you also need to understand how understanding that basics of credit will help you improve your personal credit scores. Understanding the different types of credit will help you understand the type of credit you have reporting on your credit report so you can understand what type of credit you may need to apply to help you build your credit.

Many people make the mistake of applying for the same type of credit to help them build credit and later wonder why their credit score is not improving when after several months of on time payments. Most of the time your credit score is not going to improve if you do not understand what type of credit you have and what type of credit you are going to need. Later in the book, we will discuss how your credit score is calculated. You will get a better understanding as to why understanding this is so important and how it affects the calculating your credit score. The due date. Using this method ensures that your utility bills get paid on time automatically, and if you keep the habit of paying off your credit card balance each month, your score will continue to go up. Be sure to leave the creditcards locked in a safe or drawer at home.

The fourth tip is to keep your credit card accounts open even if you are no longer charging on the card. The best policy is to keep those unused accounts open, blow the dust off your card every few months to make a small purchase, then pay it off. How long each of your accounts has been active is a major factorin your credit score.

The fifth tip is to remember that this all takes time. Following the above steps consistently over an extended period of time, will increase your credit score and allow you to qualify for betterloans and lower interest rates. Repairing your credit score does not happen overnight, so if you do these things for a few months and do not see a significant increase in your score, do not give up. They are all habits that you will want to maintain throughout your life, as they will help you to keep your finances and lines of credit under control.

Length of Time Items Can Remain on your Credit File

Delinquencies can be reported on your credit report thirty to one hundred and eighty days after the first delinquency or missed payment. A delinquent account can remain on   credit file seven years from the date of the initial missed payment.

Collection Accounts can be on tour credit report for seven years. The seven years clock starts from the date of the initial missed payment that led to the collection (the original delinquency date). When a collection account is paid, the account reports as a "paid collection" on the credit reports. Bear in mind that a paid off collection does not increase your credit score and could actually lower your credit score depending on the age of the account. If you are unsure if you should pay off a collection account you can schedule a free credit consultation phone call on our website. To speak with a board-certified credit consultant, schedule a consultation on our website at www.123creditconsultants.com.

A charge off account is another type of account that will be listed on your credit report. When a delinquent account is in collections, the account will remain on your credit for seven years. The seven-year time stamp starts from the date of the initial missed payment that led to the charge-off (the original delinquency date) even if you are making payments towards the charged-off account.

If you have a closed account, the line of credit is no longer available for further use regardless if it has a zero balance or not. A closed account that is marked as delinquent remains on your credit for seven years from the date the account is closed. Keep in mind a closed account can be closed by the consumer (you) or by the creditor.

The delinquency notation is removed seven years after the delinquency occurred. Positive closed accounts report ten years from theclosing date.

Another issue that may arise with your credit may involve a closed account. If there are no delinquencies, credit cards reported as lost will continue to be listed for two years fromthe date the creditor is contacted. Delinquent payments that occurred before the card is lost are reported for seven years.

A bankruptcy is a public record account that will be listed on your credit report under the public record section. Bankruptcy chapter seven, eleven, and twelve will remain on your credit report for ten years from the filing date. A Chapter thirteen bankruptcy is reported for seven years from the filing date. Accounts included in bankruptcy will remain for seven years from the date reported as included in the bankruptcy.

A judgement is another type of public record account that can remain on your credit file for seven years from the date filed.

Another public record that could be listed on your credit report would be a tax lien. A city, county, state, and federal tax liens could under the public records section of your credit report. Unpaid tax liensremain for fifteen years from the filing date. A paid tax lienwill remain on one's score for ten years from the date of payment.

There is another section of your credit report entitled the inquiries section. Most inquiries listed on one's credit report will continue for two years. All inquiries must continue to be fora minimum of one year from the date the inquiry is made. Some inquiries, such as employment or pre-approved offers of credit, will show only on a personal credit report pulled by you.

Information Not Allow on your Credit Report

The credit laws that were passed by Congress to protect consumers also mandates what information the credit bureaus can report about you on your credit report. Unless you provide consent, medical information cannot be reported on your credit report or provided to creditors by your doctor's office.

The credit bureaus are not allowed to report notice of a bankruptcy Chapter eleven more than ten years old, Debts (including delinquent child support payments) more than seven years old and any information regarding your personal life. The credit bureaus cannot directly report your marital status, salary, or race even if requested from a current orprospective employer.

How to Repair your Own Credit

Step 1: Order your Credit Reports

The first step to successfully repairing your credit is to obtain a copy of your credit reports. You will need one copy of your credit report from the three major credit bureaus: Transunion, Equifax, and Experian. The fourth credit bureaus, Innovis, is rather new to the market and is not being used as often as the three major credit bureaus that are mentioned previously. Therefore, we will not discuss any information about Innovis in this book.

There are two different ways that you can obtain a copy of your credit reports; you can utilize a credit monitoring service or a free resource. I will discuss both options and give you an opportunity to choose which option works best for you.

A credit monitoring service is a company that provides a copy of your credit reports AND your credit scores electronically each month. Having electronic access to your credit report and scores each month is essential to speeding up the credit restoration process. In addition to having 24/7 access to your credit report, many credit monitoring services offer you identity thief insurance and email alerts when changes have occurred on your credit reports.

If you work a full-time job, attend school, responsible for taking care of a family member, or have children then you more than likely do not have time to review three 30-40-page reports. If you choose not to have a credit monitoring services, you must review every page of your credit reports and compare them to the three 30-40- page reports that you received last month to make a note of any changes on your credit report. A credit monitoring will automatically provide you an electronic copy of your credit report, advise you of the changes, and calculate your new credit score saving you a lot of time and energy.

To choose a credit monitoring service that is the best fit for you, you will have to do your research. I highly suggest locating a company that will provide you with a credit report from all three credit bureaus, offer you electronic access, offer you identity thief insurance, and access to your credit scores monthly. To get a list of my recommended credit monitoring service you can visit: https://www.123creditconsultants.com/fcrnow

If you prefer to spend time reviewing your credit reports or if you cannot afford to pay for a credit monitoring service, you can access a free copy of your credit report by visiting www.annualcreditreport.com. The Annual Credit Report site offers you one copy of your credit report from each credit bureau once per year.

You can obtain an additional free copy of your credit report if:

1. you have been a victim of an identity thief
2. you receive welfare
3. you are denied your application for credit, insurance, or employment
4. you're unemployed and plan to look for a job within60 days

To get a credit report for free for any of the reasons listed above you will have to contact each credit bureau in writing or via phone individually to request a copy of your credit reports. Be ready to provide proof to validate your reason with a copy of the credit denial letter or letter from the welfare office.

Keep in mind that Annual Credit Report does not provide your credit scores for free only your credit reports. The credit scores are a separate price that can be purchased when you access the website. Unlike the credit monitoring services, you must pay individually for each credit score from all three credit bureaus. A credit monitoring service is usually cheaper than contacting each credit bureau separately for each credit rating.

Establishing New Credit

Before you dispute anything on your credit, make sure that you have enough open and active positive credit on your credit reports. If you do not have any credit or if you have a limited credit history, you need to establish a positive credit history by opening a new account. To understand if you have enough open and active positive credit, you must have a copy of your credit reports (see the previous step). It is hard to find a lender that will extend credit to you if you have a low credit score or if you do not have enough credit established. Many credit card companies and banks will not extend credit to you because you are considered a high-risk customer. The purpose of this section is to make sure that you have four open active, active accounts in good standing. A good rule of thumb is to ensure that you have three revolving accounts and one installment loan open, active, and in good standing.

If you have less than perfect credit, start building positive credit by applying for a secured credit card. Most secured credit card companies report your payment history to all three credit bureaus, and they do not require an excellent credit to open an account. To get a list of secured credit card recommendations and other accounts you can apply towards to boost your credit score I have a free bonus guide you can download. To gain access to your free credit score booster guide simply visit: https://www.123creditconsultants.com/creditguide.

Keep in mind that if you do not have any credit, you will more than likely pay a deposit to open a new account. The deposit is used as collateral just in case you default or don't repay the balance on yourloan or credit card.

If you have fair credit (630-675), we recommend that you apply for a card that will offer you worthwhile benefits such as mileage, points, cash back, purchase eraser, and other beneficial perks.

Be sure to make on-time payments on any account that you open. The best way to make sure you never miss or make a late payment is to set payment reminders. Keep up with your payment due dates by using the calendar on your phone, google calendars that are attached to your email, or purchase a calendar book. Many companies offer to send free reminders via email or text seven days before payment is due. You can also consider enrolling in automatic payments to have the minimum amount due debited from your bank account, credit, or debit card.

Step 2: Reviewing your Credit Reports

This is one of the most important steps in the credit repair process. DO NOT SKIP THIS SECTION! If you skip this step and moveon to the next step, you will not get the best results.

Now that you have a copy of your credit reports, it is time to move forward with step two. The second step in the credit repair process is to thoroughly review your credit reports for errors, outdated, and questionably negative accounts.

All three credit reports will provide you with your personal information, inquiries, public records, and accounts. To do an efficient job at repairing your credit, you must understand the factors that affect your FICO credit scores. The five influential factors of the FICO credit scoring model are payment history, debt ratio, length of credit history, types of credit, and number of inquiries.

35% - Payment History

A significant percentage of your score is calculated based off of your payment history. Therefore, without a positive payment history, it will be hard to obtain excellent credit. Many creditors and lenders review your credit history to see if you pay your bills on time.

If you have late payments, loan defaults, unpaid taxes, bankruptcies, and any other outstanding accounts, it will continue to lower your credit score. Starting today, make a promise to yourself to start paying your bills on time. To get exclusive access to free credit tips on how to manage and pay your bills on time, join our secret Facebook group: Credit Score Advice with 123 Credit Consultants on Facebook.

30% - Debt Ratio

Your debt ratio accounts for another big chunk of your credit score. Just because you have a credit card account open does not mean that it is helping you re-build your credit. To have excellent credit, you must learn how to manage your spending. The best rule of thumb to use is to keep your credit card balances under 30 percent of the total credit limit available. Once your credit card balances are 80 percent or above your credit cards are considered maxed out.

You can quickly boost your credit score by paying down your creditcards under 30 percent and keeping the balance low.

15% - Length of Credit History

The length of time that you have credit is important. If you have nothad an account open long enough, you will have a short length of credit age. To gain and maintain excellent credit, avoid opening unnecessary accounts and keep your current credit card accounts open even if you are not using them. Closing a credit card account can drastically change the average amount of time you have credit and drastically lower your credit score.

10% - Types of Credit

Review your credit report and make note of the type of credit you have. To achieve excellent credit, it ideal to have a mix of credit on your credit report. Many lenders like to see that you can manage different types of credit on your credit report. If you are looking to secure a mortgage, you may want to be sure that you have at least three active accounts. Many lenders like to see three active revolving accounts and one installment loan open and paid on time

10% - Number of Inquiries

The second section on your credit report will list credit inquiries. The credit inquiries section provides you details about companies who have requested to review a copy of your credit report and scores. Keep in mind that there are two different types of inquiries on your credit report.

The first type of inquiry is a hard inquiry. A hard inquiry is an inquiry that occurs when a prospective lender checks your credit report to make a lending decision. If you have recently applied to open a new account or for a new loan, the company that requested your information along with the date of the request is listed on your credit report. Hard inquiries do affect your credit, so you want to be mindful of the amount companies you allow to review your credit report.

The second type of inquiry is a soft inquiry. A soft inquiry is an inquiry that occurs when you or a company checks your credit report as a background check. Soft inquiries can appear on your credit report without your permission. However, they do not affect your credit score. Since soft inquiries do not affect your credit score, you can check your credit score and credit reports at times as often as you want.

The inquiries section on your credit report lists the hard inquiries that affect your credit. Any creditor or lender that you provide yoursocial security number to will likely review your credit report and leave a hard inquiry mark on your credit.

When you are reviewing your credit reports, keep in mind that you are reviewing them for errors. Are there any addresses listed in the personal information section of your credit report that do not recognize? Is your birthday and social security number correct? Arethere any credit inquiries listed on your credit report that you do not recognize? Do you have too many unpaid bills? Are you paying late? Did you recently file for Bankruptcy? Have you established enough credit? Ask yourself these questions as you are reviewing your credit reports. If you find any errors, inaccurate accounts, or questionably negative accounts on your credit report, highlight andcircle them.

Step 3: Sending your Disputes

C redit scores are calculated using the information that is on your credit report whether the information is accurate or inaccurate. To repair your credit, you must contact the credit bureaus directly and advise them of the information that you highlighted in the previous step. When the credit bureaus investigate the information on your credit report, they are allowed 30 days to research and 15 days to send the results of their investigation to you in the mail.

To do an efficient job at repairing your credit, you must understand the five factors that affect your FICO credit score. Be sure you understand those factors before drafting your dispute letter.

Now you are ready to send your disputes to the credit bureaus. Make sure you have the credit bureaus information handy and create a letter with your reason for the dispute. Create a letter that includes your personal data such as your name, address, phone number, SSI number, birthday and current mailing address. Make sure to include your previous address if you have been living at your current address less than 2years.

In the body of the letter, include the account/creditor name, account number, the reason for the dispute, and the action you would like the credit bureaus to take.

Be sure to include a copy of your government issued id, a current utility bill, SSI card, and copy your credit report with the account you are disputing highlighted and circled. See a sample dispute letter on the next page. Please feel free to remove the sample name and include your information.

SAMPLE CREDIT BUREAU DISPUTE LETTER

Your Name Your Address

City State and Zip Code
Telephone: (310) 111-1111
Date of Birth: 02/14/1963 SS#: 111-11-1111

Equifax Information Services LLC
P.O. Box 740256 Atlanta, GA 30374

07/04/2000

Re: Letter to Remove Inaccurate Credit Information: Report # 129854126400 To Whom It May Concern:

I received a copy of my credit report and found the following item(s) to be errors.See the attached copy of my credit report; the errors is highlighted. Here as follows are items in error:

1. Use this line to state the reason why you are disputing the account.Name of the company
   List the account number here.
   Use this link to state the action you would like the credit bureau to take.
2. Use this line to state the reason why you are disputing the account.Name of the company
   List the account number here.
   Use this link to state the action you would like the credit bureau to take.
3. Use this line to state the reason why you are disputing the account.Name of the company
   List the account number here.
   Use this link to state the action you would like the credit bureau to take.

Please send an updated copy of my credit report to the above address. Accordingto the act, there shall be no charge for this updated report. I also request that you, please send notices of corrections to anyone who received my credit report in the past six months.

Thank you for your time and help in this matter.

Sincerely,

(Sign your name on the line above)

Type or print your first and last name here.

When you are sending in your disputes make sure to begin disputing your personal information first, then dispute the negative accounts on your credit report. The credit bureau legally has 30 days to research and respond to your request and 15 days to send the response via mail. In sum, you will receive a response via U.S. mail within 30-45 days.

If you do not get a response from the credit bureaus within the time frame allotted, then you can re-submit your request via US mail anddemand that they respond to your written request. Be sure to advise the credit bureau that you will be sending a copy of this letter to the Federal Trade Commission because they are in violation of your legal right to dispute.

Step 4: Negotiate with Creditors

So, you sent off your dispute letters, and some of the items were removed and/or updated, but some accounts were marked as verified. Understand that there is a difference between an account being verified and an account being validated. When you send a letter to the credit bureaus, they are simply verifying the debt with the furnisher. When you send a dispute directly to the collection agency or furnisher, they must validate the debt.

If you have sent a dispute letter to the credit bureaus and the credit bureaus responded stating that the debt remains, you must move forward with a 'round two' dispute. A 'round two' dispute is a dispute letter sent directly to the company reporting the account on your credit report.

Negotiating with the creditors can be tricky because your verbiage can make you legally liable for the debt without you even knowing it. Make sure to avoid speaking with the creditor or collection agency over phone. They have many tricky tactics that they can use against you. The best and preferred method of communication is always via SNAIL mail aka United States Postal Service.

When the collection agency or furnisher responds back to your dispute, review the response for proper proof that you owe the debt. Simply sending a bill or letter in the mail is not offering proof that you owe the debt. Anyone can type a letter out to tell you that you owe a balance, however, simply offering a letter about the debt is not solid proof that you owe the debt.

If the collection agency provides proof that you owe the debt and that they can legally collect on the debt in your area, it is time to consider paying the past due balance. Now here is where the tricky part comes in. Paying a collection account will NOT get the account removed from your credit report. Once the collection account is paid, the collection agency does not have to remove the account from your credit report. The only responsibility the collection agency has is to contact the credit bureaus to be sure that your credit report reflects the account balance as paid in full (or settled).

To create a validation letter, you must make sure that you include enough information for the company to locate your account without providing information that they did not already have in their records. In the heading of the letter, type your full name and mailing address. Be sure to include the name of the company, the company's mailing address including the city, state, and zip code, today's date, and the account number.

In the body of your letter, explain to the company that you are requesting validation of the debt, list what consumer right that you believe they are in violation of, and mention the what action you would like to collection agency to take to resolve your request.

At the bottom of the letter be sure to include your name and signature. Send the letter to the creditor, using certified mail, so you can have a tracking number to use just in case you do not get a response from the creditor or furnisher. Do not include a copy of your government-issued identification, a copy of your social security card, or any other information regarding your identity. The creditor or furnisher should already have this information on file foryou If they are trying to collect a debt from you.

If the collection agency calls you via phone regarding your dispute letter or an account that is charged-off, kindly explain to the collection agency that you revoke your right for them to contact you via phone. In a polite tone, give the caller your mailing address and request that any information regarding the debt be sent to you in writing via mail. Do not stay on the phone with them explaining your employment status, your income, or any of your personal information to avoid admitting to the debt. Keep in mind that all most collection agencies/furnisher record all calls and they can be used against you.

Finally, avoid making payment arrangements or agreements to make a payment with the collection agency or furnisher via phone. All requests, payment arrangements, payments, etc. need to be submitted in writing so that you can keep an accurate record of when and to whom the payment was made.

Step 5: Paying Down Debt and Savings Tips

Paying down debt and learning how to save more money for emergencies is essential when you are wanting to maintain your credit score. You cannot maintain excellent credit unless you change your financial habits and patterns. Credit scores are a bi-product of your financial behavior.

The first step to repair your own credit is to dispute negative, inaccurate, and obsolete items to be removed from your credit report.

The second step is to create a plan to develop a financial plan to ensure that you do not ruin your credit score again. Do you have a plan in place for an emergency?

Improving your credit is just half of the battle. Once you get excellent credit, you must maintain it. Many people have credit troubles because they did not plan for circumstances that may happen beyond their control. What if you were laid off from your job? What if you become ill? What if you decided to get divorced? What if there is an unexpected death in the family? What if a natural disaster occurred in your hometown and you are forced to evacuate? What if you get sick and you don't have enough insurance to cover your medical procedure?

For example, what if you must have a medical procedure and your insurance policy only covers the bill AFTER you pay the deductible of $2500.00. Do you have enough money saved to pay for this emergency? What if you are in an automobile accident and you must pay your $1000 insurance deductible to get your car repaired? What if your son broke a limb at soccer practice and he needs a knee brace which is not covered by your insurance? Yes, you have insurance but what is your plan to pay when you havenot met your yearly $2500 deductible?

These questions are all hypothetical situations, but it does happen every single day. You must have a solid plan in place to prepare for unexpected emergencies, or you may end up relying on your personal credit for an emergency loan, credit line increases, and etc.

Unexpected emergencies are the number one reason why people are in so much debt and have poor credit scores. If you don't have any money saved for emergencies, then you are forced to rely on your credit. Making your emergency purchases on credit can lead tomaxed out credit cards and collection accounts for medical bills.

Paying down debt and saving must be included in your credit repair process. Paying down debt and having a "what if" savings fund for emergencies will prevent you from lowering your credit score afteryou have worked so hard to improve it.

Below are some savings tips that you can use to save for an emergency before an emergency occurs.

START SAVING FOR THE EMERGENCY BEFORE THE EMERGENCY

I know it seems impossible to save money when you have so many bills to pay, but it is not impossible. Our advisors provide our clients the tools they need to squeeze every dollar out of their budget for savings. Here are some helpful tips to remember when establishinga savings plan:

1. Start Small: Many financial advisors are taught to start off small and save 10% of their income. Put the funds in a savings account and label it "emergency funds." The goal is to have at least three paychecks saved in your emergency fund to help cover the cost of those unexpected events. Start small and continue to add any extra funds (such as overtime, bonuses, etc.) that you may receive to your savings account.

2. Automatic Debit: Are you terrible at paying yourself 1st (saving) before paying your bills? Set up an automatic direct deposit from your paycheck. You will never miss the money if you never receive it.

3. Shop Bank Rates: Pay your money in a savings account with high interest. Shop around locally or online for savings accounts that have high interest. Be careful to avoid CD accounts for emergency savings funds because you will not have access to theaccount without paying the penalty.

4. Pretend You Never Got It: So, do you remember thatbonus you have coming up or that commission/overtime/refund check you get each quarter? Use them as seed money to start saving.

Deposit it in your savings account and PRETEND YOU NEVER GOT IT. Were you paying your bills just fine before you got it right?

Step 6: Maintaining your Student Loans

You went to college and spent long hours up studying, writing papers, and sitting in class all day. You decided that you did not want to go to class anymore, dropped before half-time, or you graduated, and now you must pay your student loans. Whether you found a job using your degree, decided to go back to school until half-time, or unemployed, you are still obligated to pay your student loan(s). One of the most important factors you must remember is that they are not going away. Please do not ignore them just because you do not have the high-paying job you were hoping for in college. I made this mistake thinking that the student loan servicer would automatically know that I was not making any money and would not try to demand repayment.

What most people don't know is that student loan payments can post pond or reduced if you experienced a hardship such as a job loss, childbirth, marriage, divorce, natural disaster, and death in the family. Keep in mind that the examples listed above are not the only factors that the student loan servicer will consider. The student loan servicer can delay or post pond your student loans on a discretionary or mandatory basis. So, if your student loans are in collections, default, or just need to be paid back call and talk to the student loan servicer. Tell them about your recent hardship and allow them to help you. They have many repayment options available to assist you, but they cannot provide you with resources if you do not ask for it.

The next topic of discussion is student loan forgiveness. Now I am sure you have heard of companies offering you student loan forgiveness programs that GUARANTEE you that you will have your student loans forgiven for a small fee. Please do not believe such hype!

Student loan forgiveness programs are free. You should not be paying any third-party services for a "forgiveness program." The only way you can get a student loan forgiven is if contact your student loan servicer to ask if you qualify for any programs. Many (not all) student loan forgiveness programs require that you are employed by a city, county, state, or government level. For many of the available student loan forgiveness programs, you can hold any position if the position is approved by the student loan servicer/program. Keep in mind that government student loans are the only student loans that are eligible to be forgiven. Private student loans do not qualify for student loan forgiveness

Several student loan forgiveness programs have many requirements for you to be qualifying candidate for their program. One of those requirements is that you must make 120 on-time payments before your student loans are forgiven. To get more information about the student loan forgiveness programs, contact your student loan servicer or visit: studentaid.ed.gov.

In sum, there are several key points that you need to remember about student loan forgiveness programs. The first key point to remember is that you must apply for the forgiveness program to qualify. You do not automatically get your student loans forgiven after your 120 payments. Secondly, you must contact your student loan servicer to ask for your student loans to be on a "qualifying" repayment plan. Lastly, you must be employed at a qualifying public service organization before and while you are paying back your student loans. So, changing your employer, missing payments, and not applying for the program will prevent you from getting yourstudent loans forgiven.

New Credit Identities

Creating a new credit identity is one of the most talked about topics in the credit repair industry. You may have seen advertisements about creating a new identity (supposedly) for a fee so that you canovercome bad credit fast and have a fresh start. The answer to the question is yes you can do that but it is 100% illegal, and you can face prison time.

Many people will say no it's illegal and tell you not to do it without explaining to you how the process works. I will explain how the process works and why creating a new credit identity is illegal.

When applying for a credit card, loan, or any financing they ask youfor your social security number. The social security number is used on your credit applications to access your credit information and buyer history with the main three credit bureaus: Transunion, Equifax, and Experian. Therefore, to create a new credit identity or file, one would need a new social security number. Since it is impossible to get a new social security number from the Social Security Administration, most people sell a new identity using an Employer Identification Number (EIN) or Taxpayer Identification Number (TIN) number. Once they sell you this number, they tell you to use this number in place of your social security number, to apply for credit.

Please avoid taking this advice or using this method because this method of "credit repair" is illegal. By creating a new identity and using it to apply for a car, loans, credit cards, etc., you are committing a crime. Entering any information that is not accurate or true can be considered falsifying documents, credit card fraud, identity thief, and bank fraud. These crimes are against the law and are punishable up to years in prison, fines, and a criminal record.

Bad credit is not worth jail time. Do yourself a favor and avoid lyingon credit applications or providing inaccurate information on a credit application to because creditors will catch you. If you decidedto create a new identity instead of property repairing your credit, keep in mind that creditors have the right to provide documents to their local district attorney for prosecution.

Most people who sell "new identities" are a scam artist. If they are not scam artists, they are ignorant to the fact this method of "credit restoration" is breaking the law. Being ignorant of the law does not excuse the violations of the law. It is imperative that you understand what is and what is not legal and ethical credit restoration method. I discuss this and other illegal credit repair tactics on my Youtube show entitled: 123 Credit Tea. Go to Youtube to check out the entire episode show in detail and subscribe to my channel for more free credit tips and tricks.

Credit Repair Do's and Don'ts

DO NOT:

- Send electronic disputes
- Make payment arrangements with the collection agency without getting SOLID PROOF that you owe the debt
- Open additional accounts "just to see if you will get approved."
- Miss or skip any payments
- Close any credit card accounts you are not using.
- Open multiple cards at the same time.
- Close your credit card account (s)
- Co-sign on any loans for a friend or family member
- Purchase tradelines or CPN numbers

Do:

- Send all your disputes certified mail.
- Request information on the credit bureaus verified the account.
- Request EVERYTHING IN WRITING ... EVERYTHING!

- Set up automatic payments with your creditors.
- Review your credit report twice a year.
- Create a plan to reduce your debt.
- Create a budget.
- Subscribe to an active credit monitoring service.
- Remember that paying a collection account will not get it removed from your credit report.
- Remember credit repair takes the time it is not an overnight process.

Bear in mind that getting items removed from your credit report does not release your obligation to pay. The benefit to getting an account deleted is that no one will know that you owe that debt. However, you can still be legally liable topay or be sued.

Take time to read and understand the FDCPA, FCRA, and other laws pertaining to your rights. Remember that credit repair takes a lot of time and you must study local, state, and federal laws in your area to do an efficient job. If you would rather spend your free time with your loved ones and concentrate on earning more money, consider hiring with our credit repair consultants at 123 Credit Resolution Consultants. We provide a "Done for you Service" that allows us to do all the work for you so you can spend time doing the things that are most important to you, i.e., working, spending time with family, and managing other things in your life.

Sample Dispute Letters

Sample Dispute Letters

The sample dispute letter section of the book will provide you with sample dispute letters that you can use to challenge any questionable, negative, or obsolete items on your credit report.

Each sample dispute letters will provide you with a sample of how a dispute letter is created as well as where the letter is sent. When submitting a dispute to a credit bureau, the original creditor, or the collection agency, be sure to send your dispute certified mail.

Sending your dispute certified mail will allow you to have proof of when the dispute is sent and when it was received.

If you find that you need additional dispute letters or would to consult with me with any additional questions about your credit or financial goals, join the 123 Credit Academy. The 123 Credit Academy has online do it yourself courses to help you reach your financial goals.

The 123 Credit Academy teaches you how to repair your own credit, how save more money while still enjoying life, how to pay off debt without going broke, how to buy a home the smart way, how to build business credit, how to start your own business, and how to run your own successful business.

The 123 Credit Academy also includes bi-weekly coaching calls with me and access to a private support community. The bi-weekly coaching calls is an opportunity for you to work with me to help you with your credit and financial goals.

The private support group is also included and provides you with additional support to ask questions and work alongside of other students working towards the same goals as you. The six online courses as well as the private support group and bi-weekly coaching calls in all included in your monthly membership to the

123 Credit Academy. The academy is a paid monthly and you can cancel at any time without any cancelation fees.

As a special bonus for purchasing this book, I am giving you exclusive access to the 123 Credit Academy for fifty percent off your first month which is $23.50.

You can learn more about the 123 Credit Academy by visiting www.123creditacadmy.com and using the promo code "credit book" at checkout for a special discount off the first month.

Instructions: Use this letter to dispute any inaccurate, outdated, or obsolete information on your credit report. Be sure to send this letter to the credit bureausdirectly.

Do not include the instructions in your letter

Your First and Last Name
Your Address
Your Previous Address
Your SS# Number

Credit Bureau Name
Credit Bureau Address
Credit Bureau City, State, and Zip Code

Today's Date

Re: Letter to Remove Inaccurate Credit Information: Report # {report number}
To Whom It May Concern:
I received a copy of my credit report and found the following item(s) to be errors. See the attached copy of my credit report; the errors have been highlighted. Hereas follows are items in error:

1. Name of Company CableAccount Number Reason for Dispute
2. Name of Company CableAccount Number Reason for Dispute
3. Name of Company CableAccount Number Reason for Dispute
4. Name of Company CableAccount Number Reason for Dispute

Please send an updated copy of my credit report to the above address. According to the act, there shall be no charge for this updated report. I also request that you, please send notices of corrections to anyone who received my credit report in the past six months.

Thank you for your time and help in this matter.

Sincerely,

Your First and Last Name

Instructions: Use this letter to dispute an item on your credit report. Be sure to send this letter to the credit bureaus directly.
Do not include the instructions in your letter

Your First and Last Name
Your Address
Your Previous Address
Your SS# Number

Credit Bureau Name
Credit Bureau Address
Credit Bureau City, State, and Zip Code

Today's Date

Re: Dispute: {Account Number}. To Whom It May Concern:
I received a copy of my credit report and found the following errors. See the attached copy of my credit report; the errors have been highlighted. Here as follows is a mistake:

Account Name
Account # {if you have it}
Reason for dispute & action you would like to happen.

Account Name
Account # {if you have it}
Reason for dispute & action you would like to happen.

I am at this moment requesting that you confirm the fact that I owe this debt as required by any applicable state and federal laws. Please contact the creditor to obtain verification.

Sincerely,

Your First and Last Name

FRANCES B. WILLIAMS

Instructions: Use this letter to dispute an unauthorized inquiry on your credit report. Keep in mind that all information sent to the credit bureaus must be 100% true so only use this letter to dispute an inquiry that was not authorized by you. Be sure to send this letter to the credit bureaus directly.

***Do not include the instructions in your letter ***

Your First and Last Name
Your Address
Your Previous Address
Your SS# Number

Credit Bureau Name
Credit Bureau Address
Credit Bureau City, State, and Zip Code

Today's Date

RE: Request for Investigation of Unauthorized InquiryTo Whom It May Concern,
I checked my credit report, which I acquired from your organization on (INSERT DATE OF REPORT) and I noticed that this unauthorized inquiry had been made:

Name of CompanyInquiry Date

I contacted (CREDITOR/FURNISHERS NAME), who placed the inquiry and asked them to remove their credit inquiry from my credit profile. I also asked them to cease their illegal activities immediately, but to date, there have been no responses from their office. Since sending the letter more than 30 business daysago, they have failed to respond and honor my request.

Therefore, I must seek your help in resolving this matter. By the Fair Credit Reporting Act, I request you immediately initiate an investigation into this inquiryon my credit report to determine who authorized the inquiry. If, once your investigation is complete, you find my allegation to be correct, please remove theunauthorized inquiry from my credit report and send me an updated copy of my credit report to my address listed above.

If you do find the investigation referenced above to be valid, I request that you,please send me a full description of the procedures used in your investigation within 15 business days of the completion of the investigation.
Thank you for your help and assistance.

Sincerely,
Your First and Last Name

Instructions: Use this letter to advise creditors that you have filed for bankruptcy toavoid car repo, foreclosure, and the lien on any purchases included in your bankruptcy.
***Do not include the instructions in your letter ***

Your First and Last Name
Your Address
Your Previous Address
Your SS# Number

Credit Bureau Name
Credit Bureau Address
Credit Bureau City, State, and Zip Code

Today's Date

Re: [Company] v. [Client's first and last name] [Account Number] Balance: $XXXTo Whom It May Concern,
Please be advised that I filed a voluntary petition pursuant to Chapter 7 of the Bankruptcy Code. The bankruptcy case number is _____ and it was filed on_____withyou listed as one of my creditors.

To my knowledge, have never had non-sufficient funds and I am not aware of any negative entries. Kindly forward me a copy of my Inform Creditor for Bankruptcy record so that I may verify its accuracy.

Under 11 U.S.C. Section 362(a), you are automatically stayed by the filing of this petition from taking any action to collect any debt from me or from enforcing anylien against me. A violation of the stay may be actionable under 362(h) or as contempt of court and punishable accordingly.

Attorney name: _____
Attorney address: _____
Attorney phone number: _____

Kind regards,
Your First and Last Name

Instructions: Include Loan Modification Proposal, Hardship Letter, Monthly Expense Worksheet, Monthly Income Worksheet, Schedule of Real Estate Owned, Copy of recent mortgage statement, Copy of any delinquency notices, notice of default, or any other pertinent documents, Past 2 years tax returns, Past 2 months' pay stubs, Past 2 months bank statements, Last 6 months profit and loss (if self- employed), Copy of driver's license, 4506T - Form
***Do not include the instructions in your letter ***

Mortgage Loan Modification Request

Your First and Last Name
Your Address
Your Previous Address
Your SS# Number

Credit Bureau Name
Credit Bureau Address
Credit Bureau City, State, and Zip Code

Today's Date

Re: Loan Modification Request- 1st Mortgage Loan # (type your loan # here) To Whom It May Concern,

I am requesting a mortgage loan modification. Included with my request are supporting documentation for a loan modification regarding loan number (you're your loan number here). After reviewing my income and the current real estate market, you will find that my loan modification request is necessary. In my current situation, the mortgage payments are not affordable. However, with the proposed loan modification, I will be able to make payments on time and avoid a foreclosure consistently. I would prefer to stay in my home, but if a modification is not possible, I will be forced into foreclosure.

Please review the enclosed documents outlining my overall financial situation and real estate market conditions. You may contact me with any questions or requests for further documentation.

Sincerely,

Your First and Last Name

Consumer Resources

Additional Resources

The additional resources section of the book will provide you with contact details of recourse available to aid you in your dispute process. The additional resources are from local, state, and federal resources available tothose who would like to seek their offices for assistance.

At the time of the publication of this book, the agencies listedbelow were the truest and accurate information available.

However, I do encourage to do your research to be sure that the phone numbers, websites, and addresses are still correct before sending orcontacting these companies for assistance.

Consumer Assistance Organizations

Federal Agencies: Federal agencies enforce the various federal consumer credit laws. If you would like further information or have a credit problem that you would like addressed, you can contact theappropriate agencies. Addresses are listed below.

If your problem is with a retail department store, consumer finance company, all other creditors, and non-bank credit card issuers, credit bureaus, or debt collectors, write to:

Division of Credit PracticesFederal Trade Commission
Washington, DC 20580

If you have a problem with a national bank, write to Office of the Comptroller of the Currency Deputy Comptroller for Customer and Community Programs Department of the Treasury

6th Floor L'Enfant PlazaWashington, DC 20219

If you have a problem with a state member bank, write to Federal Reserve Board Division of Consumer and Community Affairs 20th and C Streets NWWashington, DC 20551

If you have a problem with a nonmember insured bank, or if you are uncertain of your bank's chartering (state or national), write to: Federal Deposit Insurance Corporation Office of Consumer Compliance Programs
550 17th St., NW
Washington, DC 20429

If you have a problem with a savings institution insured by the Federal Savings and Loan Insurance Corporation and a member ofthe Federal Home Loan Bank System, write to:

Federal Home Loan Bank Board Department of Consumer and CivilRights Office of
Examination and Supervision Washington, DC 20522

If you have a problem with a federal credit union, write to National Credit Union Administration Office of Consumer Affairs

1776 G St., NW
Washington, DC 20456
Many of these federal agencies have regional offices. Check your local telephone book under "United States Government" to see if there is a regional office near you.

Federal Trade Commission Offices

The Federal Trade Commission is the agency responsible for enforcing the Consumer Protection Act. If a company has violated your rights under any of these laws, you can file a complaint with the nearest regional office.

Headquarters
Pennsylvania Ave. And Sixth St., NWWashington, DC 20580

Regional Offices
1718 Peachtree St., NWAtlanta, GA 30367

10 Causeway St.
Boston, MA 02222

55 East Monroe St.
Chicago, IL 60603

8303 Elmbrook Dr.
Dallas, TX 75247

1405 Curtis St.
Denver, CO 80202

11000 Wilshire Blvd. Los Angeles, CA. 90024
26 Federal Plaza New York, NY 10278

901 Market St.
San Francisco, CA 94103

915 Second Ave.
Seattle, WA 98174

Federal Trade Commission Publications Division Washington, DC 20580

202-326-2222
www.ftc.gov

Consumer Information Websites

www.consumeraffairs.com
www.consumer.org
www.consumerlaw.org www.consumerlaw.com
www.homesaversusa.com
www.cbpp.org
www.financial-education-icfe.org/
www.pueblo.gsa.gov/crh/moneytips.htm
www.sec.gov/investor/pubs/toolkit.htm www.asec.org/
www.mymoney.gov

Consumer Federation of America is a non-profit association of
over250 pro-consumer groups with a combined membership of 50
million. Its members advance the consumer interest through
advocacy and education.
www.consumerfed.org

**Any of the following websites provide links to legal information
byspecific subject:**

www.yahoo.com/law www.law.cornell.edu/lii.table.html
www.law.indiana.edu/law/lawindex.html

Specifically, you can access a library of finance, economic and
consumer protection laws including the federal bankruptcy code
and bankruptcy rules, banking laws, Federal Trade Commission
publications and selected state consumer protection laws at:
www.pls.com:8001/his/92.htm

You can also reach various federal government sites to keep abreast of

Actions are affecting consumers. Here are just a few sites:
www.gsa.gov:80/staff/pa/cic/cic.htm(Consumer Information Center)
www.ftc.gov/

(Federal Trade Commission)
www.irs.ustreas.gov/(Internal Revenue Service)

Consumer Law Page provides the text of articles and brochures on various topics, including an article entitled "How to resolve your consumer complaint" and pamphlets published by the Federal Trade Commission, Federal Reserve Board, Comptroller of the Currency.

National Futures League and Department of Commerce. You can reach the Consumer Law Page at:
www.seamless.com/talf/tx/intro.html

The consumer group, Bankcard Holders of America, offers information on preventing credit card fraud, protecting your privacywhen using a credit card, and fending off predatory merchants.

You can reach BHA at: http://www.epn.com/bha

Interest Rates

www.ramresearch.com/

Consumer Law; Credit issues; Cards and Statute of Limitations for each

state at www.cardreport.com/lawsConsumer Action
7171 Market St., Suite 310San Francisco, Ca. 94103
415-777-9365 (Consumer complainthotline)
213-624-8327 (General hotline)

National Consumer Law Center (NCLC)18 Tremont St.
Boston, Ma. 02108
617-523-8010
www.consumerlaw.org

Ram Research Card Trak of America Consumer Information Line

460 W. PatrickSt. PO Box 1700
Frederick, Md. 21702
800-344-7714
www.cardtrak.com

Debtors Anonymous

PO Box 920888
Needham, Ma. 02492-0009
781-453-2743
www.debtorsanonymous.org

Credit Bureau's Web Address

www.equifax.com
www.transunion.com
www.experian.com
www.annualcreditreport.com

Tax Tips and Interest Rates

www.bankrate.com
www.moneycontrol.com

Renter's Rights

www.renters-rights.com
www.nolo.com
www.onlinelegalcenter.com

www.tenant.net
www.fundalarm.com

(Links to dozens of other investment sites)
www.investorama.com (Stocks, general)

www.quotesmith.com(Life insurance quotes)
www.bloomberg.com

(Business information, mortgage calculator)
www.netstockdirect.com

(Buy stocks directly from companies)Bankruptcy)
www.usdoj.gov/ust
www.abiworld.org
www.ftc.gov

Student Loans

www.loanconsolidation.ed.gov
www.salliemae.com
www.estudentlaon.com

www.studentmarket.com
www.fastweb.com

Housing

Housing Counseling (list of agencies)
www.hud.gov/hsg/sfh/hcc/hcc/ hccprofl4.cfm

Mortgages

Mortgage Bankers Association of America(Mortgages and refinancing)
1125 15th St. Washington, DC. 20005
202-861-6500
www.mbaa.org
www.irwinmortgage.com

(Mortgage information and calculator)

www.hsh.com
www.countrywide.com (Online mortgage application)
www.hud.gov
www.MortgageExpo.com
www.homepath.com

Real Estate Relocation

www.homefair.com

The Real Estate Recolcation service offers information on your new city, including the cost of living and schools. You can also create a checklist of things to do before moving day.

Career Development

www.careerbuilder.com
www.getajobservices.com
www.one-to-one-coach.com
www.jobweb.com
www.rpi.edu

Healthcare

www.maineahc.org
www.careentreeinc.com
www.qualityplans.com
www.usahealthservices.com
www.healthsavings.com

Social Services

Mental Health Counseling

Find a therapist or psychologist in yourarea
www.counseling.org
www.apa.org
www.nasw.org
www.psych.org
www.infoline.org
www.suicideassessment.com

Social Service Providers

www.apa.org
www.counseling.org
www.nasw.org
www.psych.org

www.befrienders.org

Marriage Counseling

www.divorcestopper.com
www.marriagesolutions.org
www.abuse-recovery-andmarriagecounseling.com
www.marriagematters.com
www.marriagesuccess.com

Child Support

Child Support Enforcement
370 L'Enfant Promenade SW, 4th Floor East Washington, DC
20447
(202) 401-9373
www.acf.dhhs.govOther Sites:
www.supportkids.com
www.supportguidelines.com
www.childsupportlawyer.com

Fathers' Rights

Law Offices of Jeffrey M.Leving (321) 807-3990
www.dadsrights.com

Stress Management

www.isma.org
www.ivf.com
www.mindtools.com
www.stress-management-isma.org

Substance Abuse

www.Findtreatment.samhsa.gov
www.nsawi.health.org
www.guidancechannel.com
www.drug-rehab.com

Suicide Prevention

www.spanusa.org
www.save.org
www.psycom.net
www.suicidology.org

Soldiers' and Sailors' Civil Relief Act

www.defenselink.mil/specials/Relief ActRevision
Banks and Credit UnionsNational Banks
Comptroller of the Currency Compliance Management, Mail Stop
7-5Washington, DC 20219

State Member Banks of the Reserve SystemConsumer and Community Affairs

Federal Reserve Board20th & C Streets,
NW Washington, DC20551

National Credit Union Administration

1776 G Street, NWWashington, DC 20456

Non-Member Federally Insured Banks

Office of Consumer Programs
Federal Deposit Insurance Corporation550 Seventeenth Street,
NW Washington, DC 20429

Federally Insured Savings and Loans, and Federally Chartered State
Banks Consumer Affairs Program

Office of Thrift Supervision 1700 G Street, NW Washington, DC 20552

Other Credit Card Issuers

(includes retail/gasoline companies)Consumer Response
Center Federal Trade
Commission Washington, DC 20580

Legal and Ethical Credit Repair Company

123 Credit Consultants
www.123creditconsultants.com
support@123creditconsultants.com
1-855-855-6157

Notes

Notes

Notes

Notes

Notes